Raspberry Pi Camera Controls using Python 3.2.3
For Windows and Debian-Linux
Python language, runs on most operating systems

First Edition

Herb Norbom

Author of:
Raspberry Pi Camera Controls For Windows and Debian-Linux using Python 2.7
Raspberry Pi Robot with Camera and Sound
Robot Wireless Control Made Simple with Python and C
Python Version 2.6 Introduction using IDLE
Python Version 2.7 Introduction using IDLE
Python Version 3.2 Introduction using IDLE and PythonWin
Bootloader Source Code for ATMega168 using STK500 For Microsoft Windows
Bootloader Source Code for ATMega168 using STK500 For Debian-Linux
Bootloader Source Code for ATMega328P using STK500 For Microsoft Windows
Bootloader Source Code for ATMega328P using STK500 For Debian-Linux
Books Available on Amazon and CreateSpace

Where we are aware of a trademark that name has been printed with a Capital Letter.

Table of Contents

FOREWARD..3
PREFACE..3
    Why Python?..3
PROCESS STEPS...4
    Supplies and Devices..4
    Work Directories-Raspberry Pi...4
    Setup Windows PC...5
    Setup Debian-Linux PC..5
    Program or Text Editor...5
    Python Start 5
    Testing the Pi Camera...9
    Pi Camera Module..11
        class Camera..12
        class UpdateVideoDisplay..12
        class UpdateOptionDisplay...13
        class UpdateVideoOptionDisplay..13
        setupTK(frMain)..13
        viewPicture..13
        startV...13
        cameraSTILLandVIDEOfinal32.py...15
        Remote VIDEO on Windows PC...26
THE END OR THE BEGINNING...27
APPENDIX..27
    Summary for Raspberry Pi Setup..27
    Simple DOS commands...28
    logging on to the Pi from Windows...29
    logging on to the Pi from Debian-Linux...29
    Starting Netcat and MPlayer Windows..30
    starting Netcat and MPlayer Debian-Linux...31
    PuTTY for Windows...33
    PuTTY for Debian-Linux..35
    Xming X Server for Windows...35
    Geany for Windows..37
    Geany for Raspberry Pi...37
    Netcat for Raspberry Pi and Debian-Linux...37
    Netcat for Windows..38
    Debian-Linux Shell Scripts..38
    Debian-Linux Commands..38
  Reference Sites...41
    Raspberry...41
    Raspberry - Camera..41
    Xming..41
    Python...41
    Tkinter...42
    Linux...42

FOREWARD

The Raspberry Pi is a wonderful computer. It is small and supported by a growing base of users. The Pi's small price and small footprint make it very suitable for a variety of applications. As additional hardware is made available I expect the Pi's popularity to grow. One of the recent additions to the Pi accessories is the Pi's Camera. This is small device that interfaces directly with the Pi. With the Pi's support of WiFi one can quickly visualize many applications.

PREFACE

This book grew out of my desire to appeal to people who wanted to use the Pi Camera but were not interested in the robotics application. While much of the information contained in my book Raspberry Pi Robot with Camera and Sound is included here I have expanded and focused on the Camera portion in this book. I am going to include in this book what we need to accomplish in order to operate the Camera from a remote PC running Windows or Debian-Linux; or if you just want to run the Camera from your Pi. We will write a Camera control program using Python. If you are building a robot consider the complete book and you will be able to add this program to your robot if you so desire.

As a point of reference I am currently running Microsoft Windows XP Professional Version 2002 Service Pack 3 on a Dell Dimension PC with Pentium4 CPU 3.00GHz. I am also running Debian Release 6.0.7 (squeeze) on an old PC with an Intel(R) Pentium(R) 4 CPU 2.40GHz. The Kernel Linux is 2.6.32-5-686. I am also using the GNOME Desktop 2.30.2 using the bash shell. The Raspberry Pi is running Linux Raspbian, Kernel 3.6.11, version wheezy, built from 2013-09-25-wheezy-raspbian.zip, and the Debian-Linux version is 7.2. We will use the installed Python 3.2.3 software. My home network utilizes a Netgear router.

So to get started I have listed the steps we will go through. As far as setting up the Raspberry Pi I am not going to go very far into that, but I do provide a summary in the Appendix. There are excellent sources on line, no use building a new wheel. But get the biggest SD card you can. The 4 GB just will work, but bigger is better. At this point my Pi disk is consuming less than 2 GB.

While we are going to setup the Raspberry Pi to be operational without a monitor, keyboard or mouse I suggest that as you are learning and testing that you leave those items connected.

Why Python?

Even If you have never programmed before, I suggest you start with Python. We are going to be using a lot of Python. While I am sure everyone has their own favorite programming language and good reasons for it, at this point Python is my choice. As you learn Python you will gain insight into areas you are going to need to control your robot. There are several reasons for choosing Python, they include the following:
- Object Oriented – will flow with events rather than straight lines
- Not compiled, uses an interpreter – therefore, quick results while developing applications
- Runs on Windows, Linux, Unix, even Apple – it is portable
- There is lot of FREE information on the web about it
- Python is free and already installed on your Raspberry Pi
- There are a lot of free modules - you may need to enhance your project
- What you learn, program flow and structure will to some extent carry over to C, C++ or C#, or whatever language you evolve to
- Python has a good built-in GUI, Tkinter

Yes, of course there are disadvantages, if you are going to do something for resale Python may not be the language for you. If you are here, you are probably not close to having anything to sell, so don't worry about that. Just because Python uses an interpreter do not think you are limited in terms of program size and complexity. The Raspberry Pi has multiple versions of Python installed. As of this time Python 2.7.3 is the default version. We are going to use the Python 3 which is also installed. We are going to write our programs on the Raspberry Pi and when finished we will be able to operate our Pi Camera from either a Windows PC or a Debian-Linux PC or from the Pi console. If you are not familiar with Python at all consider the book 'Python Version 3.2 Introduction using IDLE' sold on Amazon, yes I am the author, sorry about the self promoting. While I am going to provide the complete source code I am not going to go into the same depth in explaining the code as I did in my first book 'Robot Wireless Control Made Simple with Python and C'. If you are interested you can search Amazon using my name for a complete list of books.

PROCESS STEPS

- Of course you need the Raspberry Pi and various hardware items listed under Supplies and Devices. You will need to get the Pi working over a wireless communication.

- You are going to be downloading software, if you do not have a high speed connection this is going to be very difficult.

- You need to setup your directories, just makes life easier.

- We will write our Programs using Python 3.2.3 as that is installed on the Raspberry Pi and it is an excellent choice anyway. Also 'tkinter' is installed with this version of Python.

Supplies and Devices

The following parts list can be viewed as a starting point, substitute as you like. The Raspberry Pi is sold by a number of distributors. Prices shown are what I paid and they will probably have changed.

Part	Possible Source	Source Part #	Min Qty	Approx. Price	Ext. Price
Raspberry Pi Model B 512MB	AdaFruit	ID: 998	1	39.95	39.95
5V Micro USB AC Adapter	MCM	28-13060	1	6.61	6.61
Wireless N NANO USB Adapter 802.11b	MCM	831-2761	1	14.99	14.99
Raspberry Pi Camera Board	AdaFruit	ID: 805	1	29.95	29.95
Desktop High Speed USB2.0 Hub with Power Supply	Find best one. Need while testing.	Check for one working with Raspberry	1		
SD Memory Card(min4GB)	AdaFruit	many choices available	1		
SD Memory Card Reader/Writer	Find best one	very possible your computer has one	1		

I did not include a monitor, keyboard or mouse, hopefully you have spares to use while you get everything running; it is possible to run the Pi without them. We will not need them once all is working and that includes the USB Hub. For the Raspberry items in particular check out the package deals that are available. While I have used these suppliers I am not saying they are the best or the least expensive. I am not affiliated with any of them.

Work Directories-Raspberry Pi

We are going to be writing a number of programs and it can get very confusing where they are located. Also from a backup view point it is nice to have them in a separate directory. I suggest you make a separate directory now. I called my directory 'CAMERA32' in the Pi home directory. I like to keep programs for my various versions of Python in separate directories, hence the '32'.

Setup Windows PC

For our remote control we are going to need some software on the PC. There are a number of options but I am just going to list what I was able to get working. You are going to need PuTTY and Xming. PuTTY provides the communication link and Xming provides the X11 capabilities for our PC. What we are going to do is 'boot' our Raspberry Pi and then from our Windows PC log on to the Raspberry Pi. See the Appendix for downloading PuTTY and for setup. Xming is also covered in the Appendix. With everything working we will log on to the Raspberry Pi using "pi".

Setup Debian-Linux PC

If you are going to run your Pi Camera from Debian-Linux you will need to add software to the Raspberry Pi as well as to your Debian-Linux PC. While just logging in to the Pi is easy, running a GUI is a little more difficult. From a Terminal prompt on the Debian-Linux PC enter the following command:

$ ssh -X 192.168.1.9 -l pi You will need to have enabled ssh on the Pi.

Change the IP address to match where your Pi is connected. Note the capital X and the small letter L in front of Pi. See the Appendix for an illustration.

Whether you are using Debian-Linux or Windows you can run your Pi 'headless' (without a monitor). It is easier to set everything up with the Pi having a monitor, keyboard and mouse. In the Appendix I provide information and illustrations for the setup process.

Program or Text Editor

I am going to install Geany on my Raspberry Pi, on my Windows PC and on the Debian-Linux PC, see the Appendix for installation information. You can use any text editor you like, that includes Python's Idle, nano, vi or vim or whatever you like. Each has pluses and minuses. A very nice feature of Geany is that you can run the program right from Geany. Once you are running the program remotely or as they say 'headless' with no monitor attached you may appreciate this feature.

Python Start

The following walks you through your first Python program using a Windows PC. The process for running from Debian-Linux is similar to the Windows process. See the Appendix for getting this working. Once you are logged onto the Pi from either the Windows PC or the Debian-Linux PC the process becomes the same because you are running from the Pi.

First let us make a very small Python program. I have installed Geany on the Raspberry Pi and I have logged onto the Raspberry Pi from my Windows PC using PuTTY, log-in as pi. I have Xming running on the PC at this point. I suggest you change to our CAMERA32 directory. Enter from the command prompt

'cd /home/pi/CAMERA32' or if in the pi home directory just 'cd CAMERA32'. (See Illustration1)

Before we write our first program script I suggest you type 'python3' at the # prompt. If all is well you should get a message from Python. Mine says Python 3.2.3 (default, Mar 1, 2013....) and gives the Python prompt of >>>.

If you get the Python prompt you can enter "Crtl z" to exit Python and return to the # prompt.

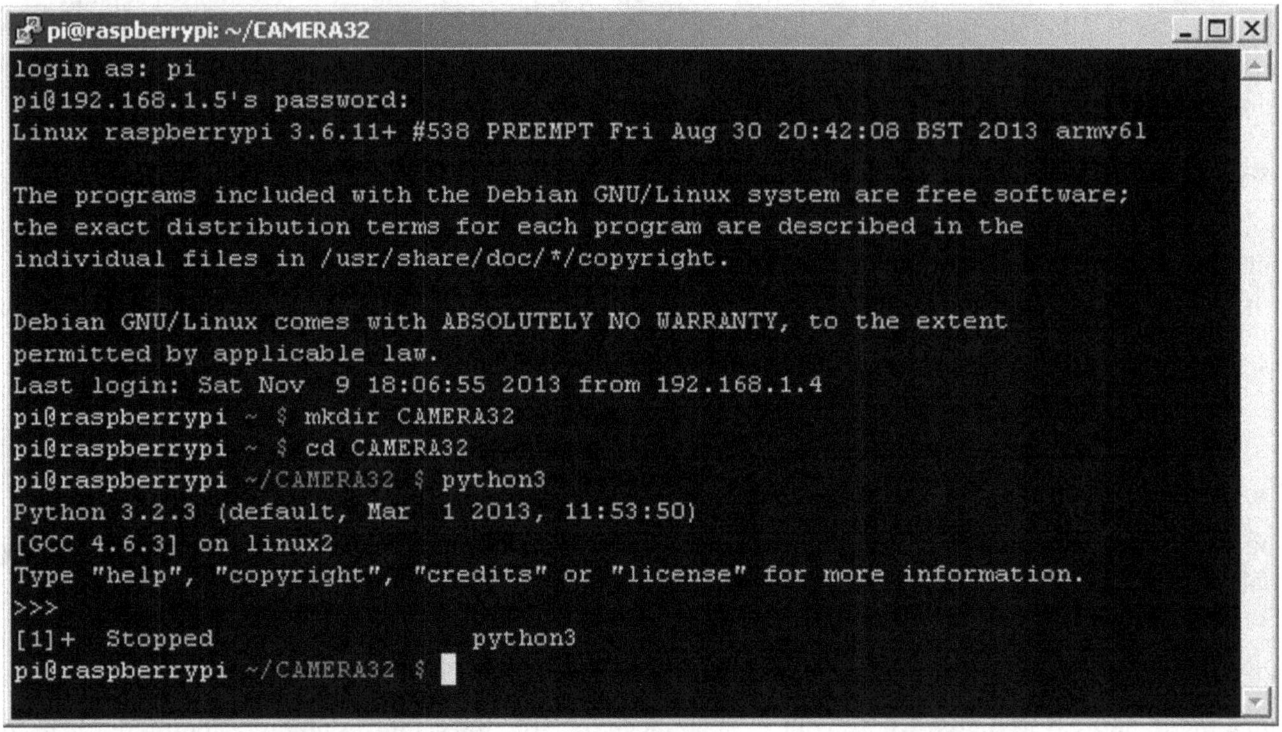

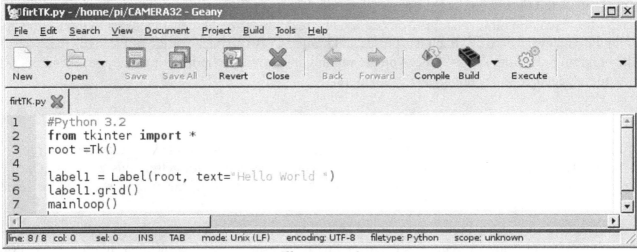

Illustration 1

With Python working let us write our first script using Geany. (You will need to have Xming working, see Appendix for that installation.) Enter 'geany' at the # prompt. Go ahead and enter the program code and save file as 'firstTK.py'. The 'py' extension is required by Python and Geany also uses it to identify the script type.

Illustration 2

One of the many nice things about Geany is that you can execute the script without leaving Geany. First let us make sure that the execute command in Geany is correct. Click on 'Build' and select 'Set Build Commands'. Under the last items on the screen you will probably see Execute as python "%f". That is the only command we are interested in at this point. (The "%f" is your program name that Geany enters automatically for you.) Note that it is calling Python and not Python3. You have a choice you can change that command to python3"%f" or as I have done add another Execute commands as #2. I called mine EXprompt and set it as python3"%f" as shown in Illustration3. The disadvantage to doing as I did is that you need to select 'Build' from the top menu and the EXprompt. I went this way because I still have a lot of Python2.7 programs and found it a little easier to keep track of what I was running.

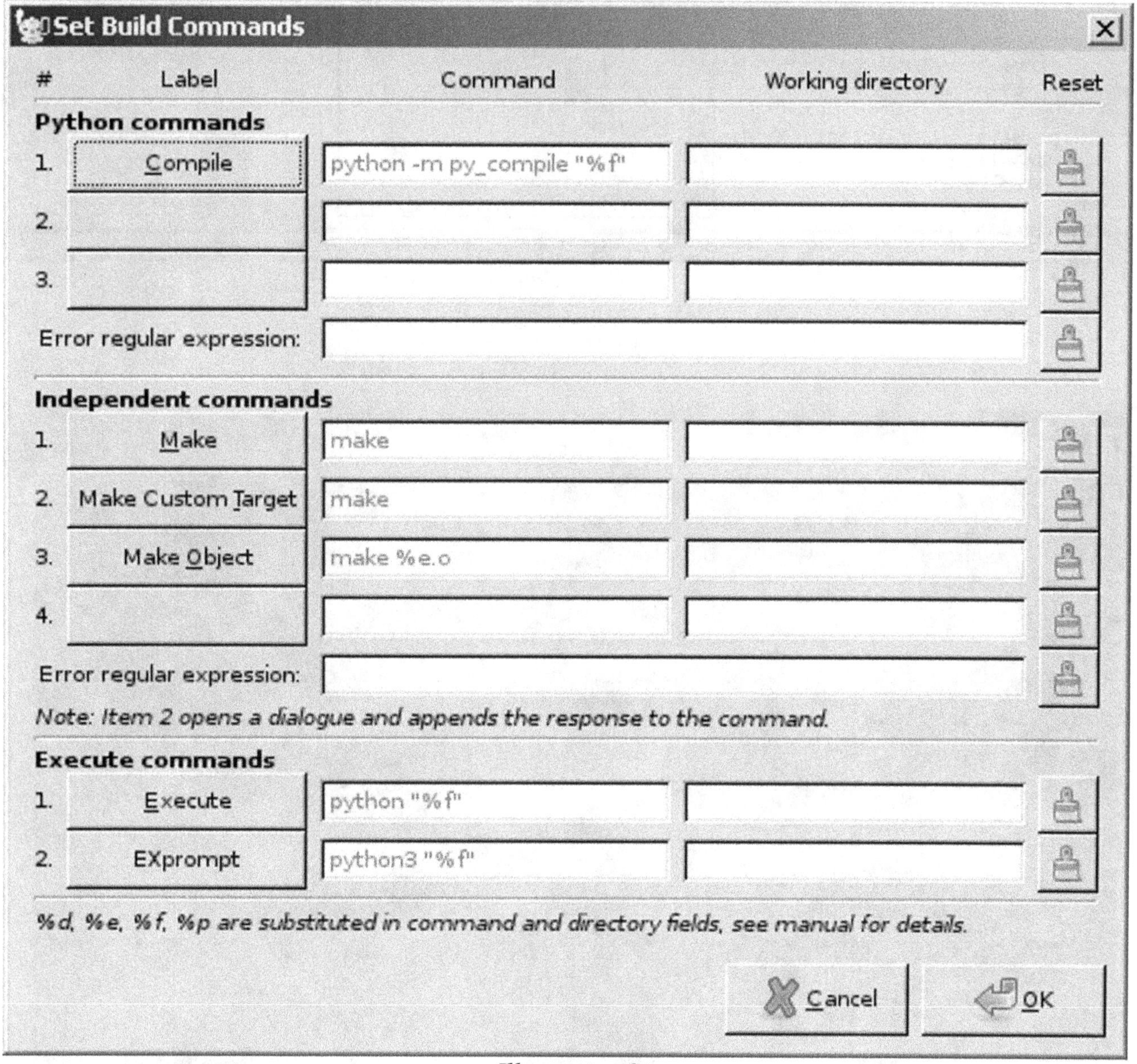

Illustration 3

Click OK or Cancel to close the window.

To run the Python script using EXpromt, click on '<u>B</u>uild' and select 'EXprompt' as shown in Illustration4. If you changed the Execute button to python3 you can simply click on Execute. Either way will result in a LXTerminal window opening and our tkinter window will be open on it.

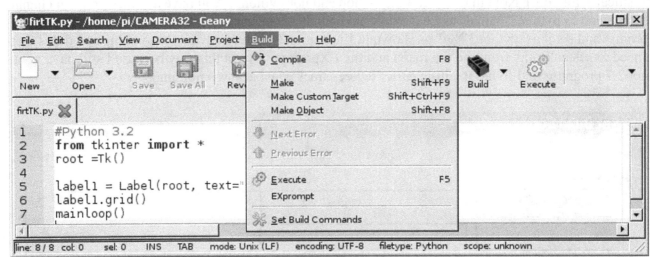

Illustration 4

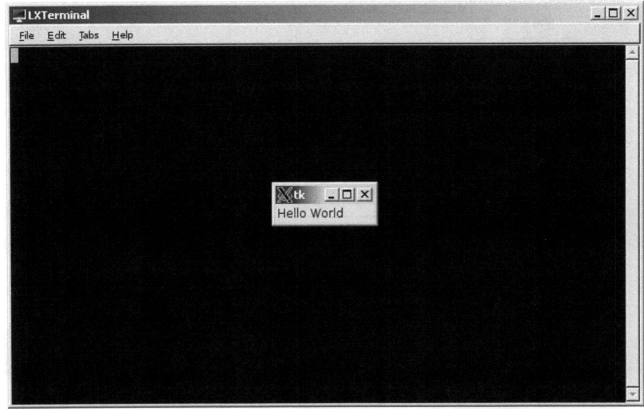

Illustration 5

Our tkinter window also shows. This works like a normal window, click on the x to close. When you close the tkinter window the LXTerminal window will prompt you with the message "Press return to continue", the LXTerminal closes when you press return.

If you had problems with this you may want to try running directly from your Raspberry Pi console. We need to have this working before proceeding. If you can, take some time and explore the features of Geany.

If you want to run from the Pi console you can. Geany needs to have X windows running. If you are running from Gnome or LXDE you may see Geany on the menu. If not there select LXTerminal and run from that window by typing 'geany'.

I am sure you are aware, but just in case I need to mention how to shutdown your Pi. You should always run a 'shutdown' procedure. These procedures ensure an orderly closing of files and help prevent corruption of your SD. A good procedure is "shutdown -h now", if not logged in as root, precede the command with "sudo". On the Pi Gnome Desktop GUI there is a shutdown icon.

Testing the Pi Camera

We can do some simple commands from the terminal prompt to ensure that the camera is working. The first one will be to see if the Pi Camera help is available. I will be running the examples from my Windows PC. I am using PuTTY and Xming.

Enter   "raspivid -?"   (Note in all the commands for the camera spacing is important.)

```
pi@raspberrypi: ~/CAMERA32                                              _ |□| x|
pi@raspberrypi ~/CAMERA32 $ raspivid -?
Display camera output to display, and optionally saves an H264 capture at req
uested bitrate


usage: raspivid [options]

Image parameter commands

-?, --help        : This help information
-w, --width       : Set image width <size>. Default 1920
-h, --height      : Set image height <size>. Default 1080
-b, --bitrate     : Set bitrate. Use bits per second (e.g. 10MBits/s would be -
b 10000000)
-o, --output      : Output filename <filename> (to write to stdout, use '-o -')
-v, --verbose     : Output verbose information during run
-t, --timeout     : Time (in ms) to capture for. If not specified, set to 5s. Z
ero to disable
-d, --demo        : Run a demo mode (cycle through range of camera options, no
capture)
-fps, --framerate      : Specify the frames per second to record
-e, --penc        : Display preview image *after* encoding (shows compression a
rtifacts)
-g, --intra       : Specify the intra refresh period (key frame rate/GoP size)

Preview parameter commands

-p, --preview     : Preview window settings <'x,y,w,h'>
-f, --fullscreen      : Fullscreen preview mode
-op, --opacity    : Preview window opacity (0-255)
-n, --nopreview   : Do not display a preview window
```

Illustration 6

```
 pi@raspberrypi: ~/CAMERA32                                        _ □ X

Image parameter commands

-sh, --sharpness          : Set image sharpness (-100 to 100)
-co, --contrast : Set image contrast (-100 to 100)
-br, --brightness         : Set image brightness (0 to 100)
-sa, --saturation         : Set image saturation (-100 to 100)
-ISO, --ISO      : Set capture ISO
-vs, --vstab     : Turn on video stablisation
-ev, --ev        : Set EV compensation
-ex, --exposure  : Set exposure mode (see Notes)
-awb, --awb      : Set AWB mode (see Notes)
-ifx, --imxfx    : Set image effect (see Notes)
-cfx, --colfx    : Set colour effect (U:V)
-mm, --metering  : Set metering mode (see Notes)
-rot, --rotation         : Set image rotation (0-359)
-hf, --hflip     : Set horizontal flip
-vf, --vflip     : Set vertical flip
-roi, --roi      : Set region of interest (x,y,w,d as normalised coordinates [
0.0-1.0])


Notes

Exposure mode options :
off,auto,night,nightpreview,backlight,spotlight,sports,snow,beach,verylong,fi
xedfps,antishake,fireworks

AWB mode options :
off,auto,sun,cloud,shade,tungsten,fluorescent,incandescent,flash,horizon

Image Effect mode options :
none,negative,solarise,sketch,denoise,emboss,oilpaint,hatch,gpen,pastel,water
colour,film,blur,saturation,colourswap,washedout,posterise,colourpoint,colour
balance,cartoon

Metering Mode options :
average,spot,backlit,matrix

pi@raspberrypi ~/CAMERA32 $
```

Illustration 7

With this working let's try the commands to display a picture and then a short video. To display a picture on the console enter the following: "raspistill -w 400 -h 400". On occasion the console will start displaying improper characters. If that happens you can enter "reset" at the prompt. Let's try a short video display on the console. At the terminal prompt enter "raspivid -w 400 – h 400". Both commands are shown in the following illustration.

Illustration 8

You can play with entering the various options shown from the Help command given earlier. While entering commands from the prompt or from a script file works, I wanted more. I wanted a program that could control the camera. Make changes on the fly to make a video or take a still picture; configure the various options; and save pictures or videos. With these goals in mind I wrote the following program that I hope is not too convoluted. I had planned to provide two programs, one for video and one for still pictures. As I went through the development it became clear that the majority of the options applied to both types. So for better or worse one program it is. While I do like to develop applications in modules I did not find that to be of benefit here, you may feel differently as the program is getting a little on the long side.

Pi Camera Module

The goal of this module is to have camera defaults set and to be able to adjust the settings from our Python program. In some of my other books I go into more depth on some of the standard modules we will be using, but there is a wealth of information on the web also. If you happened to have followed my book "Raspberry Pi Robot with Camera and Sound" you will quickly see that this program is based on the camera module included in that book. This program has a great many more options. In fact I have tried to include as many as I thought applicable. The program is driven by the options that you select. Your first decision is to select the picture type, STILL or VIDEO. From there you can make your selections in any order you like. The Pi Camera has lots of options that are fun to play with in combinations. To help visualize the program the following illustration shows the control window.

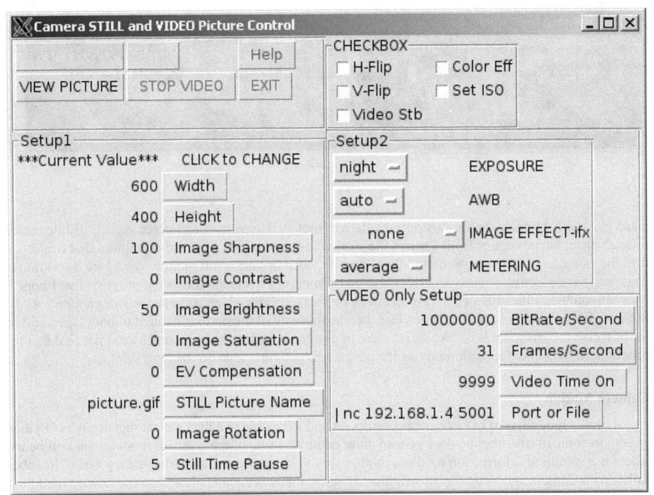

Illustration 9

The framing or groupings on the window are primarily driven by the type of choices each offers. Where the choice is only VIDEO I have put that in a separate frame. As you get into the program you will hopefully note and maybe even agree that I have used variable names that are intuitive to the process. I have tried to place comments in the program to help me to remember and you to see what I am trying to accomplish.

class Camera

After all the imports are coded I set up our first class, the class Camera. We will create two instances of the class one for display and one to work with. This method makes it a little easier to update the display when changes are made to our variables. We will have two instances of the class Camera: SELF and DISP. I have used the same values in setting up both instances

class UpdateVideoDisplay

We are also going to create a class for UpdateVideoDisplay. In this class we use labels and buttons for making desired changes. Within this class I have setup a FRAME, you can see Illustration 9 the text is 'Setup1'. Within this class we also setup a function 'def videoChange(DISP)' to update the Labels of our display. We call this function when we want to update our display. Following this class I have added the functions that are called when a variable is changed.

class UpdateOptionDisplay

This class UpdateOptionDisplay is used to contain the items that I used an "OptionMenu" to offer the valid choices. You will note I have tried to include all the available options for each item. On Illustration9 you can see the Frame text as 'Setup2', I called the Frame 'combFr' as it will hold this class and the next one.

class UpdateVideoOptionDisplay

The class UpdateVideoOptionDisplay is used to control VIDEO only options. The control and updating procedure is the same type used for our first class. The items for the display and option choices are included in the Frame name 'Setup2'. After the Labels and variable displays the functions that are called are shown.

setupTK(frMain)

Because I want this program to run as an import or independently we use the "if __name__ =='__main__':" procedure. If you run the program from a prompt or directly from Geany the program 'knows' to execute the 'main' and the items below it. If we call the program, after importing it, we will call a function of the program. If you are not familiar with this I hope the fog lifts as you work through the program. When you run from the prompt the program will of course do it's normal checking and setup, but it will run the function setupTk(1) as its first step. I have set a switch to indicate where the program is being run from, if run independently I want to set up a normal Tk() window, you may think of it as the root or master window. If run or import from a separate program I want to make the window a Toplevel window; as I do not want to have two master or root windows running.

I have added a Frame to keep our Buttons organized. Most of the Buttons are standard buttons, you click them and they call a function and run accordingly. The exception is the Button which I have set equal to B1. This button determines if you are selecting a VIDEO or STILL camera action. When you click the button a function is called like the other Buttons. Within the function some interesting items are looked at. The function looks at what the 'text' of the button is set at and changes to the opposite. If it was VIDEO it will change to STILL. This took me a fair amount of time to get working, but once understood the concept can be applied to any button and its configuration options.

Also included in this section are 'Checkbuttons'. These are just on/off type selections. Yes they are also placed in a Frame, shown on Illustration9 as 'CHECKBOX'.

Near the end of this section the 'combFr is defined, note we use this Frame for two of the classes described earlier.

The last two items are just to run the earlier described functions.

viewPicture

This function is different from the other functions. You can use this to list the 'gif' files in a directory and to view the gif format pictures. As I wanted to stick to standard pictures that Python could display without going obtaining additional modules, only 'gif' formatting is shown. You can look at other Python modules, 'pil' for example for other formats. When you have selected a 'gif' picture it will be displayed on the screen you are running this program from.

startV

This is the function that actually sends the command to the Pi Camera. Needless to say it is the meat of the program. You will probably quickly note that the vertical and horizontal flip options are treated differently than other options. I could not get them to work when I listed them by themselves. So of course I cheated a little. I made a short decision tree and tacked them on to the back of the 'rotation' option as needed. Having a good thing working I continued the 'tacking' on process as needed for visual stabilization, color effect and ISO. While on the subject of ISO, I am not sure how ISO works with the Pi Camera. I could not see any difference when the option was on or off. But what do I know so I left it in the program.

You may have noticed that I have setup STILL pictures to be saved to a file on the Pi Raspberry. After the picture is saved you can view it on your PC or on the Raspberry Pi. For the VIDEO you can stream the video to your PC, view it on the Raspberry Pi OR save it to a file on the Raspberry Pi. The video format needs to be 'h264' format. To view the video file on the Raspberry Pi you can run 'omxplayer' from a Pi terminal prompt. If you want to copy the file to your PC I suggest you use a USB drive, NetCat, Samba or other file transfer utility. You can also setup to save the VIDEO on your Pi. Be aware if saving the VIDEO file on your Raspberry Pi that the files can get quite large very quickly.

The actual command sent to the Pi Camera depends on your selection of STILL or VIDEO. For STILL I use the subprocess Popen and have set the process equal to 'p'. I can then obtain the 'pid' and tell the process to wait until finished.

For VIDEO the process is very similar to the STILL process with the exception of NOT including the 'wait' instruction. Leave it off so you can click on the 'STOP VIDEO' button shown in Illustration9.

For VIDEO I define the port or file that you want to send the video to. (You will need to have downloaded Netcat for the Raspberry Pi and the Windows or Linux-Debian PC that you plan to use as your control. You will also need to use a video player on the machine you want to display the video on. I am using MPlayer, see appendix for notes on installing that as well and Netcat.) Note the spacing of the commands and the line continuation character '\'. If you have been playing with the camera you may have had some problems stopping the video. As we are using the subprocess function to start the camera we can easily capture its 'pid', (process identifier). Once we have that we can issue a 'kill' command to stop the process.

If you are running the program from the Raspberry Pi console the video will display on the console, and you will not need Netcat or MPlayer for that purpose. But once we start running remotely you will need them.

When you get to the point of running the program, you will need to start the Netcat program on your PC first. You will see this running in your DOS or command prompt window. Getting Netcat and the MPlayer software running takes some time. You will at some point notice a very noticeable lag between what the camera sees and what is displayed on your screen. This is a result of writing to the cache and reading from the cache. The procedure uses a first in first out from the cache. Try just a short run with the camera on, click stop video, let the cache empty then restart the video. I hope that you get decent results; my delays went away doing this.

The following screen shots are the complete Python program for controlling your Pi Camera. I generally like to give the reader the chance to build the program in blocks so that the debugging process is a little easier. The program works fine, but you will find that spacing is critical. This program did not lend itself to that practice. As you look at the code you may want to try to break down the process into creating the 'classes' one at a time. A lot of the code you enter can be copied, pasted and then edited to save a few keystrokes. Whichever way you go the following is the code. You can of course use whatever name you like for the program, just use the 'py' extension.

cameraSTILLandVIDEOfinal32.py

```
cameraSTILLandVIDEOfinal32.py - /home/pi/CAMERA32 - Geany

File  Edit  Search  View  Document  Project  Build  Tools  Help

cameraSTILLandVIDEOfinal32.py

 1    # Control Program for Raspberry Pi camera
 2    # using Python 3.2.3   setup to run on Linux
 3    # author Herb  11/9/2013 company RyMax, Inc. www.rymax.biz
 4    # for personal hobby use only, include references to RyMax Inc. for
 5    # resale or commercial use contact RyMax, Inc. for written persmission.
 6    from tkinter import *
 7    from tkinter.filedialog import askopenfilename
 8    import tkinter.simpledialog
 9    import os
10    import subprocess
11    import signal
12
13    class Camera:
14        def __init__(DATA,picType,width,height,sharpness,contrast,brightness,
15            saturation,evCompensation,pictureName,rotation,sTime,
16            vBitrate,vTime,vFps,vPort):
17            DATA.picType=picType
18            DATA.width=width
19            DATA.height=height
20            DATA.sharpness=sharpness
21            DATA.contrast=contrast
22            DATA.brightness=brightness
23            DATA.saturation=saturation
24            DATA.evCompensation=evCompensation
25            DATA.pictureName=pictureName
26            DATA.rotation=rotation
27            DATA.sTime=sTime
28            DATA.vBitrate=vBitrate
29            DATA.vTime=vTime
30            DATA.vFps=vFps
31            DATA.vPort=vPort
32    SELF = Camera(
33        'STILL',                 #Picture type will be STILL or VIDEO
34        600,                     #display width
35        400,                     #display height
36        100,                     #sharpness
37        0,                       #contrast
38        50,                      #brightness
39        0,                       #saturation
40        0,                       #EV Compensation
41        "picture.gif",           #picture file name
42        0,                       #rotation
```

```
line: 327 / 492   col: 17    sel: 0    INS   TAB    mode: Win (CRLF)    encoding: UTF-8    filetype: Python    scope: setupTk
```

Illustration 10

Raspberry Pi Camera Controls using Python 3.2.3   Page 15

File   Edit   Search   View   Document   Project   Build   Tools   Help

cameraSTILLandVIDEOfinal32.py ✖

```
43              5,                      #still time pause before picture in ms
44              10000000,               #video bit rate 10MBits
45              9999,                      #video time in ms
46              31,                     #video frames per second
47              '| nc 192.168.1.4 5001')   #video default output port for VIDEO
48                                      #remote using NetCat
49      #for DISP setting same as SELF
50      DISP = Camera('',600, 400, 100,0,50,0,0,"picture.gif",0,5,
51              10000000,9999,31,'| nc 192.168.1.4 5001')
52      class UpdateVideoDisplay():
53          def __init__(DISP):
54              DISP.vFr = LabelFrame(TOP, width =40, height=118,
55              bd=2, text='Setup1', relief=GROOVE)
56              DISP.vFr.grid(column =0,row=1,sticky=(N,W,S))
57              Label(DISP.vFr, text='***Current Value***').grid(column=0,row=1)
58              Label(DISP.vFr, text='    CLICK to CHANGE').grid(column=1,
59                  row=1,sticky=(W))
60          #width
61              DISP.width = StringVar()
62              DISP.width.set(SELF.width)
63              Label(DISP.vFr,textvariable=DISP.width).grid(column=0,
64                  row=2,sticky=(E))
65              Button(DISP.vFr,text="Width",command=imWidth).grid(column=1,
66                  row=2,sticky=(W))
67          #height
68              DISP.height = StringVar()
69              DISP.height.set(SELF.height)
70              Label2=Label(DISP.vFr, textvariable=DISP.height)
71              Label2.grid(column=0, row=3, sticky=(E))
72              Button(DISP.vFr,text="Height",command=imHeight).grid(column=1,
73                  row=3,sticky=(W))
74          #sharpness
75              DISP.sharpness = StringVar()
76              DISP.sharpness.set(SELF.sharpness)
77              Label(DISP.vFr,textvariable=DISP.sharpness).grid(column=0,
78                  row=4,sticky=(E))
79              Button(DISP.vFr,text="Image Sharpness",command=sharpnessSet).grid(
80                  column=1,row=4,sticky=(W))
81          #contrast
82              DISP.contrast = StringVar()
83              DISP.contrast.set(SELF.contrast)
84              Label(DISP.vFr,textvariable=DISP.contrast).grid(column=0,
```

line: 327 / 492   col: 17   sel: 0   INS   TAB   mode: Win (CRLF)   encoding: UTF-8   filetype: Python   scope: setupTk

Illustration 11

```
 85              row=5,sticky=(E))
 86          Button(DISP.vFr,text="Image Contrast",command=contrastSet).grid(
 87              column=1,row=5,sticky=(W))
 88      #brightness
 89          DISP.brightness = StringVar()
 90          DISP.brightness.set(SELF.brightness)
 91          Label(DISP.vFr,textvariable=DISP.brightness).grid(column=0,
 92              row=6,sticky=(E))
 93          Button(DISP.vFr,text="Image Brightness",command=brightnessSet).grid(
 94              column=1,row=6,sticky=(W))
 95      #saturation
 96          DISP.saturation = StringVar()
 97          DISP.saturation.set(SELF.saturation)
 98          Label(DISP.vFr,textvariable=DISP.saturation).grid(column=0,
 99              row=7,sticky=(E))
100          Button(DISP.vFr,text="Image Saturation",command=saturationSet).grid(
101              column=1,row=7,sticky=(W))
102      #evCompensation
103          DISP.evCompensation = StringVar()
104          DISP.evCompensation.set(SELF.evCompensation)
105          Label(DISP.vFr,textvariable=DISP.evCompensation).grid(column=0,
106              row=8,sticky=(E))
107          Button(DISP.vFr,text="EV Compensation",command=evCompensationSet).grid(
108              column=1,row=8,sticky=(W))
109      #pictureName
110          DISP.pictureName = StringVar()
111          DISP.pictureName.set(SELF.pictureName)
112          Label(DISP.vFr,textvariable=DISP.pictureName).grid(column=0,
113              row=9,sticky=(E))
114          Button(DISP.vFr,text="STILL Picture Name",
115              command=pictureNameSelect).grid(column=1,row=9,sticky=(W))
116      #rotation
117          DISP.rotation = StringVar()
118          DISP.rotation.set(SELF.rotation)
119          Label(DISP.vFr,textvariable=DISP.rotation).grid(column=0,
120              row=10,sticky=(E))
121          Button(DISP.vFr,text="Image Rotation",command=rotationSet).grid(
122              column=1,row=10,sticky=(W))
123      #still time pause
124          DISP.sTime = StringVar()
125          DISP.sTime.set(SELF.sTime)
126          Label(DISP.vFr,textvariable=DISP.sTime).grid(column=0,
```

Illustration 12

Raspberry Pi Camera Controls using Python 3.2.3   Page 17

File   Edit   Search   View   Document   Project   Build   Tools   Help

cameraSTILLandVIDEOfinal32.py ✖

```
127  ┤                      row=11,sticky=(E))
128  ⊟          Button(DISP.vFr,text="Still Time Pause",command=sTimeSet).grid(
129  ┤                      column=1,row=11,sticky=(W))
130
131  ⊟      def videoChange(DISP):
132             DISP.width.set(SELF.width)
133             DISP.height.set(SELF.height)
134             DISP.contrast.set(SELF.contrast)
135             DISP.sharpness.set(SELF.sharpness)
136             DISP.brightness.set(SELF.brightness)
137             DISP.saturation.set(SELF.saturation)
138             DISP.evCompensation.set(SELF.evCompensation)
139             DISP.pictureName.set(SELF.pictureName)
140             DISP.rotation.set(SELF.rotation)
141             DISP.sTime.set(SELF.sTime)
142
143  ⊟def imWidth():
144  ⊟      temp=tkinter.simpledialog.askinteger("Enter integer for width",
145             "Between 100 & 1920: ",
146  ┤          initialvalue=SELF.width,minvalue=100,maxvalue=1920)
147  ⊟      if temp != None:
148  ┤          SELF.width=temp
149  └      UpdateVideoDisplay()
150  ⊟def imHeight():
151  ⊟      temp=tkinter.simpledialog.askinteger("Enter integer for height",
152             "Between 50 & 1080: ",
153  ┤          initialvalue=SELF.height,minvalue=50,maxvalue=1080)
154  ⊟      if temp != None:
155  ┤          SELF.height=temp
156  └      UpdateVideoDisplay()
157  ⊟def sharpnessSet():
158  ⊟      temp=tkinter.simpledialog.askinteger("Enter integer for sharpness",
159             "Between -100 & 100:",
160  ┤          initialvalue=SELF.sharpness,minvalue=-100,maxvalue=100)
161  ⊟      if temp != None:
162  ┤          SELF.sharpness=temp
163  └      UpdateVideoDisplay()
164  ⊟def contrastSet():
165  ⊟      temp=tkinter.simpledialog.askinteger("Enter integer for contrast",
166             "Between -100 & 100:",
167  ┤          initialvalue=SELF.contrast,minvalue=-100,maxvalue=100)
168  ⊟      if temp != None:
```

line: 327 / 492   col: 17   sel: 0   INS   TAB   mode: Win (CRLF)   encoding: UTF-8   filetype: Python   scope: setupTk

Illustration 13

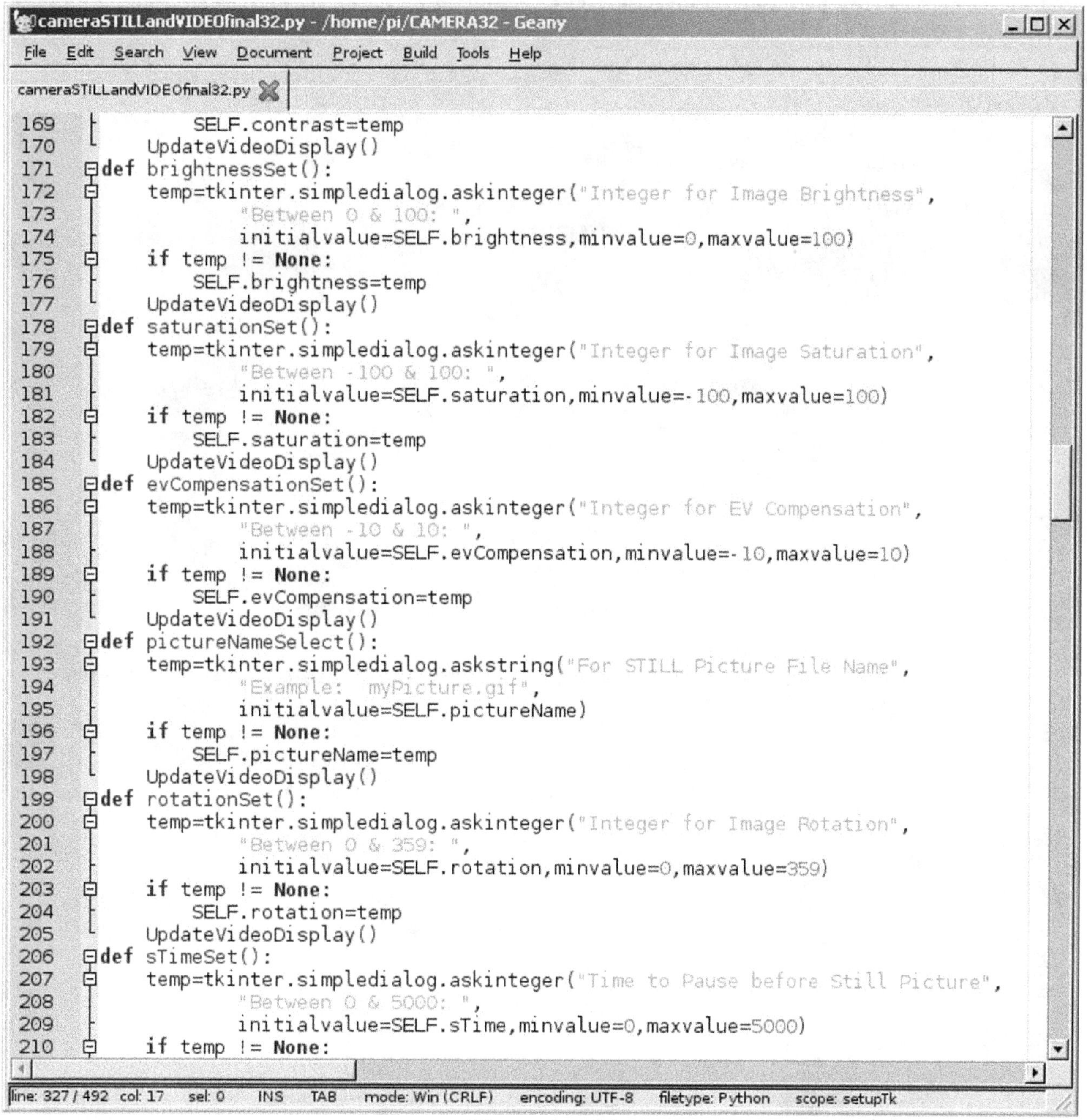

```
169          SELF.contrast=temp
170       UpdateVideoDisplay()
171 def brightnessSet():
172    temp=tkinter.simpledialog.askinteger("Integer for Image Brightness",
173          "Between 0 & 100: ",
174          initialvalue=SELF.brightness,minvalue=0,maxvalue=100)
175    if temp != None:
176       SELF.brightness=temp
177    UpdateVideoDisplay()
178 def saturationSet():
179    temp=tkinter.simpledialog.askinteger("Integer for Image Saturation",
180          "Between -100 & 100: ",
181          initialvalue=SELF.saturation,minvalue=-100,maxvalue=100)
182    if temp != None:
183       SELF.saturation=temp
184    UpdateVideoDisplay()
185 def evCompensationSet():
186    temp=tkinter.simpledialog.askinteger("Integer for EV Compensation",
187          "Between -10 & 10: ",
188          initialvalue=SELF.evCompensation,minvalue=-10,maxvalue=10)
189    if temp != None:
190       SELF.evCompensation=temp
191    UpdateVideoDisplay()
192 def pictureNameSelect():
193    temp=tkinter.simpledialog.askstring("For STILL Picture File Name",
194          "Example:  myPicture.gif",
195          initialvalue=SELF.pictureName)
196    if temp != None:
197       SELF.pictureName=temp
198    UpdateVideoDisplay()
199 def rotationSet():
200    temp=tkinter.simpledialog.askinteger("Integer for Image Rotation",
201          "Between 0 & 359: ",
202          initialvalue=SELF.rotation,minvalue=0,maxvalue=359)
203    if temp != None:
204       SELF.rotation=temp
205    UpdateVideoDisplay()
206 def sTimeSet():
207    temp=tkinter.simpledialog.askinteger("Time to Pause before Still Picture",
208          "Between 0 & 5000: ",
209          initialvalue=SELF.sTime,minvalue=0,maxvalue=5000)
210    if temp != None:
```

line: 327 / 492   col: 17   sel: 0   INS   TAB   mode: Win (CRLF)   encoding: UTF-8   filetype: Python   scope: setupTk

Illustration 14

File   Edit   Search   View   Document   Project   Build   Tools   Help

cameraSTILLandVIDEOfinal32.py ✕

```
211              SELF.sTime=temp
212          UpdateVideoDisplay()
213
214  class UpdateOptionDisplay():
215      global exposure, awb, ifx, metering
216      def __init__(DISP):
217          DISP.oFr = LabelFrame(combFr, width =30, height=118,
218          bd=2, text='Setup2', relief=GROOVE)
219          DISP.oFr.grid(column =0,row=0,sticky=(N,W,S))
220      #exposure
221          exposure.set('night')
222          Label(DISP.oFr,text="EXPOSURE").grid(column=1,row=8,sticky=(W))
223          OptionMenu(DISP.oFr,exposure,'off','auto','night','nightpreview',
224              'backlight','spotlight','sports','snow','beach','verylong',
225              'fixedfps','antishake','fireworks',).grid(column=0,
226              row=8,sticky=(W))
227      #awb
228          awb.set('auto')
229          Label(DISP.oFr,text="AWB").grid(column=1,row=9,sticky=(W))
230          option= OptionMenu(DISP.oFr,awb,'off','auto','sun',
231              'cloud','shade','tungsten','fluorescent','incandescent',
232              'flash','horizon').grid(column=0,row=9, sticky=(W))
233      #ifx
234          ifx.set('none')
235          Label(DISP.oFr,text="IMAGE EFFECT-ifx").grid(column=1,row=10,sticky=(W))
236          option= OptionMenu(DISP.oFr,ifx,'none','negative','solarise',
237              'sketch','denoise','emboss','oilpaint','hatch','gpen',
238              'pastel','watercolor','film','blur','saturation','colorswap',
239              'washedout','posterise','colorpoint','colorbalance',
240              'cartoon')
241          option.config(width=10)
242          option.grid(column=0,row=10, sticky=(W,E))
243      #metering
244          metering.set('average')
245          Label(DISP.oFr,text="METERING").grid(column=1,row=11,sticky=(W))
246          option= OptionMenu(DISP.oFr,metering,'average','spot',
247              'backlit','matrix').grid(column=0,row=11, sticky=(W))
248
249  class UpdateVideoOptionDisplay():
250      global exposure, awb, ifx, metering
251      def __init__(DISP):
252          DISP.vFr = LabelFrame(combFr, width =40, height=118,
```

line: 327 / 492   col: 17   sel: 0   INS   TAB   mode: Win (CRLF)   encoding: UTF-8   filetype: Python   scope: setupTk

Illustration 15

File   Edit   Search   View   Document   Project   Build   Tools   Help

cameraSTILLandVIDEOfinal32.py

```
253                    bd=2, text='VIDEO Only Setup', relief=GROOVE)
254              DISP.vFr.grid(column =0,row=1,sticky=(N,W,S,E))
255        #bitrate
256              DISP.vBitrate = StringVar()
257              DISP.vBitrate.set(SELF.vBitrate)
258              Label(DISP.vFr,textvariable=DISP.vBitrate).grid(column=0,
259                    row=0,sticky=(E))
260              Button(DISP.vFr,text="BitRate/Second",command=bitrate).grid(column=1,
261                    row=0,sticky=(W))
262        #fps
263              DISP.vFps = StringVar()
264              DISP.vFps.set(SELF.vFps)
265              Label(DISP.vFr,textvariable=DISP.vFps).grid(column=0,
266                    row=1,sticky=(E))
267              Button(DISP.vFr,text="Frames/Second",command=imfps).grid(column=1,
268                    row=1,sticky=(W))
269        #videoTime
270              DISP.vTime = StringVar()
271              DISP.vTime.set(SELF.vTime)
272              Label(DISP.vFr,textvariable=DISP.vTime).grid(column=0,
273                    row=2,sticky=(E))
274              Button(DISP.vFr,text="Video Time On",command=vTime).grid(column=1,
275                    row=2,sticky=(W))
276        #port
277              DISP.vPort = StringVar()
278              DISP.vPort.set(SELF.vPort)
279              Label(DISP.vFr,textvariable=DISP.vPort).grid(column=0,
280                    row=3,sticky=(E))
281              Button(DISP.vFr,text="Port or File",command=portSelect).grid(column=1,
282                    row=3,sticky=(W))
283        def video2Change(DISP):
284              DISP.vBitrate.set(SELF.vBitrate)
285              DISP.vFps.set(SELF.vFps)
286              DISP.vTime.set(SELF.vTime)
287              DISP.vPort.set(SELF.vPort)
288    def bitrate():
289        temp=tkinter.simpledialog.askinteger("Enter integer for BitRate",
290              "Example 10,000,000 for 10MBits",initialvalue=SELF.vBitrate)
291        if temp != None:
292              SELF.vBitrate=temp
293        UpdateVideoOptionDisplay()
294    def imfps():
```

line: 327 / 492   col: 17   sel: 0   INS   TAB   mode: Win (CRLF)   encoding: UTF-8   filetype: Python   scope: setupTk

Illustration 16

Raspberry Pi Camera Controls using Python 3.2.3   Page 21

```
295        temp=tkSimple.Dialog.askinteger("Enter integer for fps",
296            "Between 5 & 50:\
297            \if you change May need to change nc also",
298            initialvalue=SELF.vFps,minvalue=5,maxvalue=50)
299        if temp != None:
300            SELF.vFps=temp
301        UpdateVideoOptionDisplay()
302 def vTime():
303        temp=tkinter.simpledialog.askinteger("Integer for Video Time On",
304            "Between 999 & 99999999: ",
305            initialvalue=SELF.vTime,minvalue=999,maxvalue=99999999)
306        if temp != None:
307            SELF.vTime=temp
308        UpdateVideoOptionDisplay()
309 def portSelect():
310        temp=tkinter.simpledialog.askstring("Enter Port or filename.h264",
311            "Example 192.168.1.6 5001 or video.h264",
312            initialvalue=SELF.vPort)
313        if temp != None:
314            SELF.vPort=temp
315        UpdateVideoOptionDisplay()
316
317 def setupTk(frMain):
318        global TOP
319        if frMain==1:            #program run as stand alone
320            TOP = Tk()
321        if frMain==0:            #program imported & run from other Python script
322            TOP = Toplevel()
323        TOP.title( "Camera STILL and VIDEO Picture Control" )
324        TOP.geometry( "545x380+40+90" ) #width, height, placement x  y
325        bFr=LabelFrame(TOP, width=218, height=50,bd=2, relief=GROOVE)
326        bFr.grid(column=0,row=0,sticky=(N,W,E,S))
327        Button(bFr,text="START CAMERA",fg='green',width=9,command=startV).grid(
328            column=0,row=0,sticky=W)
329        global B1
330        B1=Button(bFr,text=SELF.picType,fg='green',width=3,command=setTYPE)
331        B1.grid(column=1,row=0,sticky=W)
332        Button(bFr,text="Help",fg='brown',command=helpV).grid(column=2,row=0,
333            sticky=W)
334        Button(bFr,text="VIEW PICTURE",fg='black',width=9,command=viewPicture).grid(
335            column=0,row=1,sticky=W)
336        Button(bFr,text="STOP VIDEO",fg='red', command=stopV).grid(column=1,row=1,
```

Illustration 17

```
337              sticky=W)
338          Button(bFr,text="EXIT", fg='red', command=exitCamera).grid(column=2,row=1,
339              sticky=W)
340     #define Checkbuttons for various items that are on or off
341     #define Frame for Checkbutton
342          DISP.cFr = LabelFrame(TOP, width =50, height=50,
343              bd=2, text='CHECKBOX', relief=GROOVE)
344          DISP.cFr.grid(column =1,row=0,sticky=(N,W))
345          global v1, v2, v3,v4,v5
346          v1 = IntVar()
347          v2 = IntVar()
348          v3 = IntVar()
349          v4 = IntVar()
350          v5 = IntVar()
351          C1 = Checkbutton(DISP.cFr,text='H-Flip', variable=v1)
352          C1.grid(column=0,row=0,sticky=W)
353          C2 = Checkbutton(DISP.cFr,text='V-Flip', variable=v2)
354          C2.grid(column=0,row=1,sticky=W)
355          C3 = Checkbutton(DISP.cFr,text='Video Stb', variable=v3)
356          C3.grid(column=0,row=2,sticky=W)
357          C4 = Checkbutton(DISP.cFr,text='Color Eff', variable=v4)
358          C4.grid(column=1,row=0,sticky=W)
359          C5 = Checkbutton(DISP.cFr,text='Set ISO', variable=v5)
360          C5.grid(column=1,row=1,sticky=W)
361          UpdateVideoDisplay()
362          global exposure, awb, ifx, metering
363          exposure=StringVar()
364          awb=StringVar()
365          ifx=StringVar()
366          metering=StringVar()
367          global combFr   #Frame for holding the frames Setup2 and VIDEO Only Setup
368          combFr = LabelFrame(TOP, width =200, height=118)
369          combFr.grid(column=1, columnspan=3,row=1,sticky=(N,W,S,E))
370          UpdateOptionDisplay()
371          UpdateVideoOptionDisplay()
372
373     def setTYPE():
374          print(B1.configure('text'))        #left these print statments in to
375          myText= B1.configure('text')       #show structue of data
376          if myText[4]=='STILL':
377              SELF.picType="VIDEO"
378              B1.configure(text='VIDEO')
```

Illustration 18

```
379          B1.configure(fg='green')
380      if myText[4]=='VIDEO':
381          SELF.picType="STILL"
382          B1.configure(text='STILL')
383          B1.configure(fg='blue')
384
385  def viewPicture():
386      try:
387          fileToView=askopenfilename(filetypes=[("gif",".gif")])
388          print (fileToView)
389          viewTop = Toplevel()                    #create child window
390          viewTop.geometry("610x420+600+90")   #width, height, placement x   y
391          viewTop.title("GIF picture viewer")
392      except:
393          print ('error on viewTop window')
394      try:
395          image = PhotoImage(file=(fileToView),width =600, height=400 )
396      except:
397          print ('image problem')
398      try:
399          v=fileToView
400          picframe = LabelFrame(viewTop, text=v,borderwidth=4, relief="sunken",
401              width=605, height=405)
402          picframe.grid(column=0, row=0, sticky=(N,W,E,S))
403          picLabel=Label(picframe, image = image)
404          picLabel.grid(column=0, row =0, sticky=W)
405          picLabel.image = image
406      except:
407          print('error loading image file')
408
409  def startV():
410      global p, preexec_fn, exposure
411      pexposure=exposure.get()
412      print ('pexposure' , pexposure)
413      pawb=awb.get()
414      pifx=ifx.get()
415      pmetering=metering.get()
416      hFLIP=v1.get()
417      vFLIP=v2.get()
418      dispSET=''             #not sure why, but have to build set or hf & hv
419      if ((hFLIP == 1) & (vFLIP==1)):          #don't work
420          dispSET = ' -rot '+str(SELF.rotation)+' -hf --hflip -vf --vflip'
```

Illustration 19

Raspberry Pi Camera Controls using Python 3.2.3   Page 24

File   Edit   Search   View   Document   Project   Build   Tools   Help

cameraSTILLandVIDEOfinal32.py ✖

```
421     if ((hFLIP == 0) & (vFLIP==1)):
422         dispSET = ' -rot '+str(SELF.rotation)+' -vf --vflip'
423     if ((hFLIP == 0) & (vFLIP==0)):
424         dispSET = ' -rot '+str(SELF.rotation)
425     vSTAB=v3.get()
426     if vSTAB==1:
427         dispSET = dispSET+' -vs --vstab'
428     colEFF=v4.get()
429     if colEFF==1:
430         dispSET = dispSET+' -cfx --colfx'
431     capISO=v5.get()
432     if capISO==1:
433         dispSET = dispSET+' -ISO --ISO'
434     print ('dispSET: ',dispSET)
435     if SELF.picType=='STILL':
436         camStill = 'raspistill -w '+str(SELF.width)\
437             +' -h '+str(SELF.height)\
438             +' -e gif' \
439             +' -sh '+str(SELF.sharpness)\
440             +' -co '+str(SELF.contrast)\
441             +' -br '+str(SELF.brightness)\
442             +' -sa '+str(SELF.saturation)\
443             +' -ev '+str(SELF.evCompensation)\
444             +' -ex '+str(pexposure)\
445             +' -t '+str(SELF.sTime)\
446             +' -awb '+str(pawb)\
447             +' -ifx '+str(pifx)\
448             +' -mm '+str(pmetering)\
449             +dispSET\
450             +' -o '+str(SELF.pictureName)
451         p = subprocess.Popen(camStill, shell=True, preexec_fn=os.setsid )
452         print ('Child PID: ', p.pid)
453         print (camStill)
454         p.wait()            #need to wait until subprocess completes
455     if SELF.picType=='VIDEO':
456         camVideo = 'raspivid -w '+str(SELF.width)\
457             +' -h '+str(SELF.height)\
458             +' -sh '+str(SELF.sharpness)\
459             +' -co '+str(SELF.contrast)\
460             +' -br '+str(SELF.brightness)\
461             +' -sa '+str(SELF.saturation)\
462             +' -ev '+str(SELF.evCompensation)\
```

line: 327 / 492   col: 17   sel: 0   INS   TAB   mode: Win (CRLF)   encoding: UTF-8   filetype: Python   scope: setupTk

Illustration 20

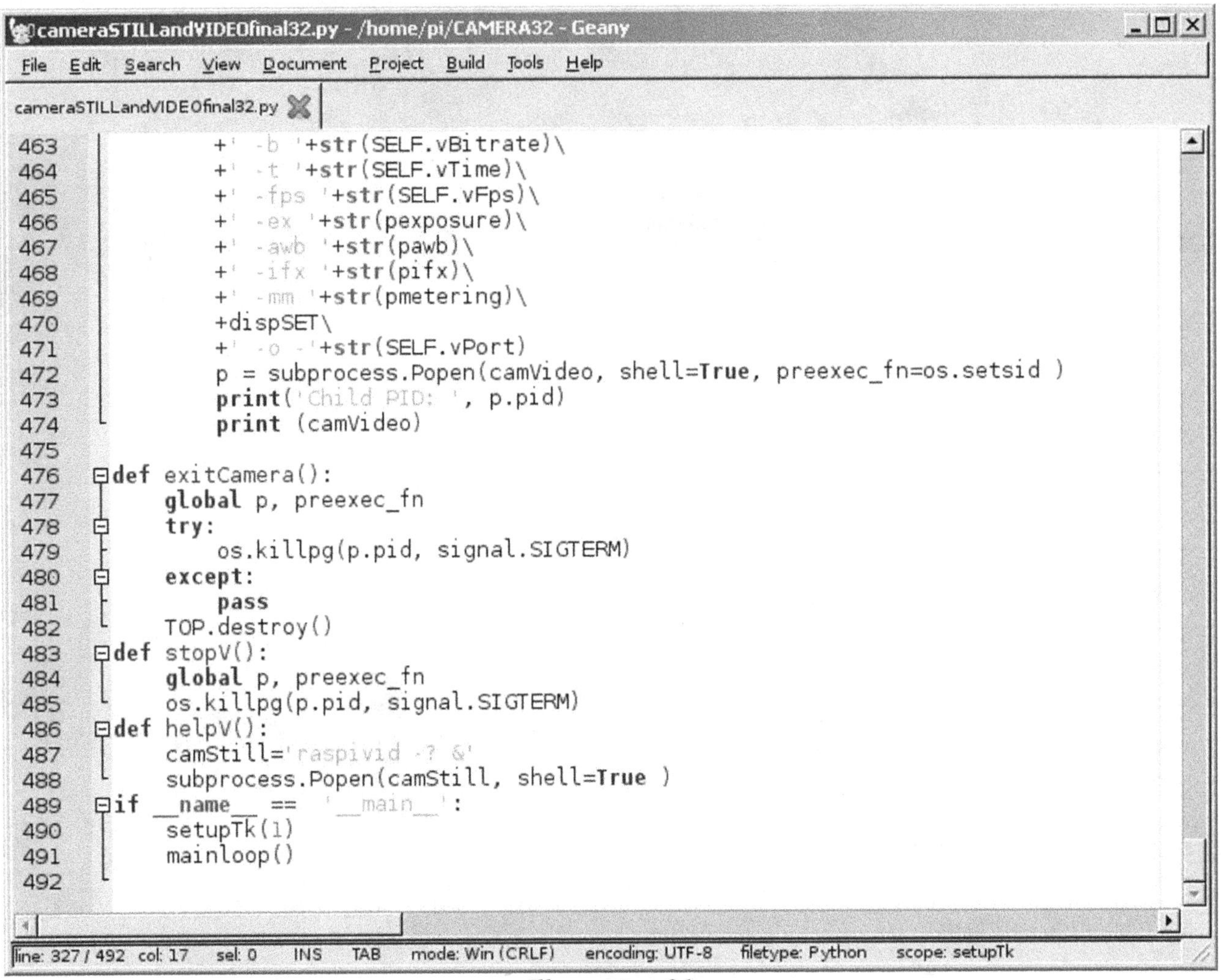

```
463                +' -b '+str(SELF.vBitrate)\
464                +' -t '+str(SELF.vTime)\
465                +' -fps '+str(SELF.vFps)\
466                +' -ex '+str(pexposure)\
467                +' -awb '+str(pawb)\
468                +' -ifx '+str(pifx)\
469                +' -mm '+str(pmetering)\
470                +dispSET\
471                +' -o '+str(SELF.vPort)
472            p = subprocess.Popen(camVideo, shell=True, preexec_fn=os.setsid )
473            print('Child PID: ', p.pid)
474            print (camVideo)

476     def exitCamera():
477            global p, preexec_fn
478            try:
479                os.killpg(p.pid, signal.SIGTERM)
480            except:
481                pass
482            TOP.destroy()
483     def stopV():
484            global p, preexec_fn
485            os.killpg(p.pid, signal.SIGTERM)
486     def helpV():
487            camStill='raspivid -? &'
488            subprocess.Popen(camStill, shell=True )
489     if __name__ == '__main__':
490            setupTk(1)
491            mainloop()
492
```

line: 327 / 492   col: 17   sel: 0   INS   TAB   mode: Win (CRLF)   encoding: UTF-8   filetype: Python   scope: setupTk

Illustration 21

Now that you have all the coding done, time to run. IF in Geany select your "CameraSTILLandVIDEOFINAL32.py" and select 'Execute' if you changed the command. Or select 'Build' and 'EXpromt' that was added. Or if you are running from a command prompt enter

"python3 CameraSTILLandVIDEOFINAL32.py".

Remote VIDEO on Windows PC

On the Windows PC I set up the following bat file to start Netcat and MPlayer. I saved Netcat and MPlayer in My Documents directory. To run them I set up a batch file in the 'netcat' directory. See the Appendix for instructions on downloading Netcat and MPlayer. The following is the simple bat file I created to get it running. You can setup a similar script on the Debian-Linux PC if you like; remember to make it executable if using Debian-Linux.

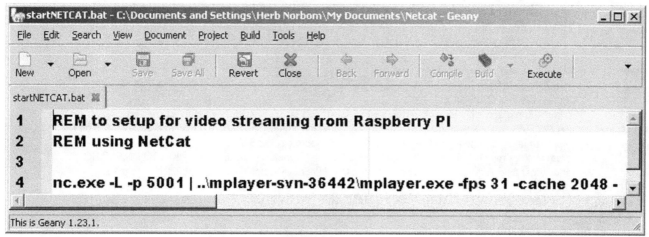

Illustration 22

THE END OR THE BEGINNING

I hope that you have learned a lot and had some fun.

Visit the web site www.rymax.biz for additional information. I would like to learn from your experience, you can e-mail me at herb@rymax.biz.

APPENDIX

Summary for Raspberry Pi Setup

There is a good chance that the steps taken to setup your Raspberry Pi will evolve over time. The following is just a guide as to the steps that I took. While I did build a new OS for this book, you need to expect things to change, and of course I may have forgotten something, but I don't think so. Check out the web for the latest instructions.

Raspberry pi building the SD card	
	I have settled on the debian-wheezy with the desktop that is standard with it LXDE
	I have used the pc as the source and a desktop running debian-wheezy -linux.
	download the file from
see	http://www.raspberrypi.org/downloads
see	http://elinux.org/RPi_Easy_SD_Card_Setup
	same for either pc on linux
	under file manager double click on the file to unzip 2012-12-16-wheezy-raspbian.zip
Download image 2013-09-25-wheezy-raspian.zip file 577 Mb Version wheezy Kernel 3.6 FILE size 605,227,145 on MY PC Disk	
	this then is used to generate the image file which is approx 2,892,800 KB
	from Prompt run sha1sum on the img file 2013-09-25-wheezy-raspian.img PRIOR TO UNZIPPING
	should get following Raspberry Pi download page 99e6b5e6b8cfbf66e34437a74022fcf9744ccb1d
	takes a few minuets to run MAKE SURE YOU RUN ON THE ZIP FILE
	I got 99e6b5e6b8cfbf66e34437a74022fcf9744ccb1d 2013-09-25-wheezy-raspbian.img
Download SD Formatter 4.0 sor SD/SDHC/SDXC	
	https://www.sdcard.org/downloads/formatter_4/
	I installed My Documents\SDFormatter It put Icon on Desktop
Make sure you set FORMAT SIZE ADJUSTMENT to ON in the Options menu	
	http://elinux.org/RPi_Hardware_Basic_Setup
Disk Image Win32	
	down load from
	http://sourceforge.net/projects/win32diskimager/
Insert SD in Raspberry Pi and power up the Raspberry Pi	
	should boot to raspi-config
	select EXPAND-ROOTFS -Expand Root Partion to Fill SD Card I did not want a separate partition
	then let it reboot should now be able to see full size
	login pi
	pwd raspberry
	sudo raspi-config
	change password for pi
	sudo passwd pi
	enter new password twice
	enable SSH under advanced options
	exit raspi-config
	sudo apt-get update
	sudo apt-get upgrade
	suggest a reboot
	login pi
	sudo raspi-config
	enable camera
	A good idea to run again
	sudo apt-get update
	sudo apt-get upgrade
	suggest a reboot
	login pi
	if you want to start desktop startx

Illustration 23

Simple DOS commands

Before we go any further, a few quick words on DOS commands. They can do damage, they are not very user friendly; they will destroy without asking twice. So make sure the command you enter is the command that you want and that you know what the command is going to do.
Simple DOS commands, execute from the DOS command prompt. Remember DOS is not case sensitive.

- Dir or dir   – This will give you the contents of the current directory

- Help   – all the commands that are available
- Help dir   – gives you all the options available with dir
- cd {dir name} – change directory, you would add the directory name
- cd ../   – moves up the directory tree one level
- cls   –clear the DOS window screen

logging on to the Pi from Windows

Make sure you have started the Xming server. You need to start PuTTY and use the settings shown for PuTTY. You will log-in as 'pi'. PuTTY will display the Pi's log-in window. See the Appendix sections for setting up PuTTY and Xming.

Illustration 24

logging on to the Pi from Debian-Linux

There are a lot of ways to do this, the following is the simplest method I have found to enable a GUI interface, have a video feed and log-in as the user pi. You must have ssh enabled on the Pi. You probably have already set this. You can check by entering on the Pi the following command sudo raspi-config and looking at the Advance Options, A4 and making sure that SSH is enabled.

From a terminal prompt on your Debian-Linux PC enter the command "ssh -X 192.168.1.9 -l pi". As I mentioned earlier make sure you use a capital X and a small letter L. You will be asked for the pi password. As you can see in the Illustration I changed to our program directory and started Geany.

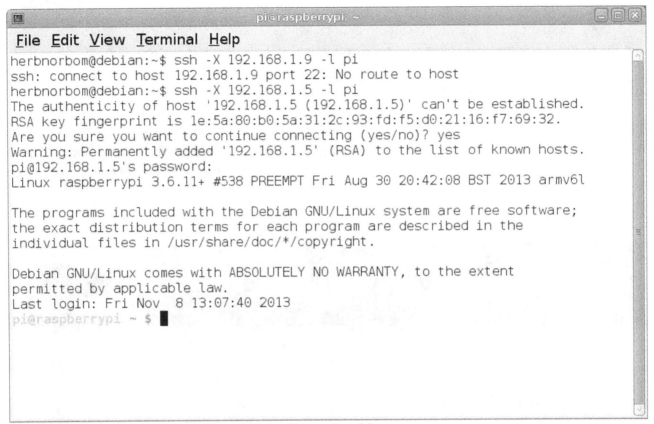

Illustration 25

As you can see from Illustration25 I did not have the correct IP address the first try. The second time I get an RSA warning, no not from NSA. Just accept and you will not get the warning the next time. Now that you are logged on to the Raspberry Pi, change directory to CAMERA32 and you can type geany and select your program and run it.

Starting Netcat and MPlayer Windows

We are only using DOS to start our Netcat program. I am going to create a bat script in the location where my '*cmd*' prompt opened. Adjust the following as needed for your system.

Use a simple text editor, Geany or the DOS edit program to create a simple bat file for starting the video capture. At this point I have downloaded and installed Netcat and MPlayer. In my case both were installed in directories under "My Documents" adjust the bat file or script as needed. But what the script or bat file does is change to the directory where I installed Netcat and issue a list directory command. I then put a second bat file in that directory to actually start Netcat and display the video. While you can combine the two bat files if you like, I kept them separate because I kept playing with the options on the second one and was tired of changing directories. My first bat file is named "raspberryFeed.bat" and it is saved in the directory where the command or DOS prompt opens. It only has two lines, so if you are good at remembering where things are you may not need this bat file. The two lines are:
cd My Documents\Netcat
dir

The second bat file is really the more important one as I will not remember the command to start Netcat. This bat file is named startNETCAT.bat and I saved it in the Netcat directory.(see Illustration26) I just have

one line, you can adjust for example fps, but seems to work best if it matches what you set the camera program at. You can also play with the cache size. For Windows this is the command that I use:
nc.exe -L -p 5001 | ..\mplayer-svn-36442\mplayer.exe -fps 31 -cache 2048 -

nc.exe is the Netcat program
-L   is for Windows only, instructs program Listen harder, or a persistent listener, like NSA
-p 5001 is the local port that I want to listen to
| the vertical line is the pipe command, what Netcat hears we pipe to mplayer.exe
..\mplayer-svn-36442   is the directory that I installed mplayer.exe in
mplayer.exe   is the program that displays the video that Netcat hears
-fps   frames per second
-cache   size (you can play with and try various sizes)
     –   need this last dash to make it work

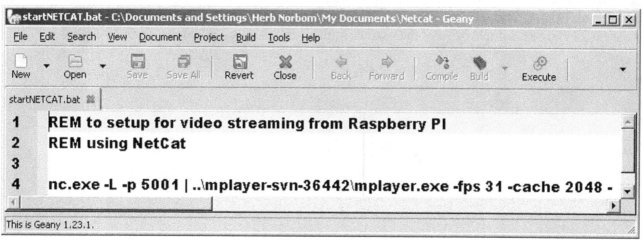

Illustration 26

To end the program use "Ctrl c".

To test you can run the script on the Windows PC. On the Pi you need to start the camera with the command "raspivid -t 9999 -o - | nc 192.168.1.4 5001". Note the IP address is the IP for the Windows PC. A good reference site is: http://www.raspberrypi.org/camera .

starting Netcat and MPlayer Debian-Linux

The start-up is very similar to the Windows version. From a terminal prompt on the Debian-Linux PC I entered the following command which I have saved in a script file. Remember to make your script file executable. That is a small letter L after nc.

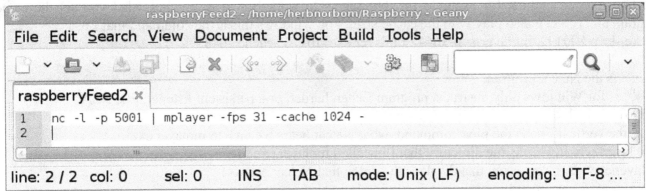

Illustration 27

To test you can run the script in Illustration27 on the Debian-Linux PC. On the Pi you need to start the camera with the command "raspivid -t 9999 -o - | nc 192.168.1.6 5001". Note the IP address is the IP for the Debian-Linux PC. A good reference site is: http://www.raspberrypi.org/camera .

Illustration 28 shows a sample of what the output on the Debian-Linux PC looks like.

```
┌──────────────────────────────────────────────────────────────────────────┐
│ ▣              herbnorbom@debian: ~/Raspberry                    □ ⊡ ⊠    │
├──────────────────────────────────────────────────────────────────────────┤
│ File  Edit  View  Terminal  Help                                           │
│ herbnorbom@debian:~/Raspberry$ . raspberryFeed2                          ▲ │
│ MPlayer SVN-r31918 (C) 2000-2010 MPlayer Team                            │ │
│ Can't open joystick device /dev/input/js0: No such file or directory     │ │
│ Can't init input joystick                                                │ │
│ mplayer: could not connect to socket                                     │ │
│ mplayer: No such file or directory                                       │ │
│ Failed to open LIRC support. You will not be able to use your remote control. │
│                                                                          │ │
│ Playing -.                                                               │ │
│ Reading from stdin...                                                    │ │
│ Cache fill: 19.53% (204800 bytes)                                        │ │
│                                                                          │ │
│ Cache not filling!                                                       │ │
│ Cache not filling!                                                       │ │
│ Cache not filling!                                                       │ │
│ Cache not filling!                                                       │ │
│ Cache not filling!                                                       │ │
│ Cache not filling!                                                       │ │
│ Cache not filling!                                                       │ │
│ Cache not filling!                                                       │ │
│ Cache not filling!                                                       │ │
│ Cache not filling!                                                       │ │
│ Cache not filling!                                                       │ │
│ Cache not filling!                                                       │ │
│ Cache not filling!                                                       │ │
│ H264-ES file format detected.                                            │ │
│ Cache not responding!                                                    │ │
│ open: No such file or directory                                          │ │
│ [MGA] Couldn't open: /dev/mga_vid                                        │ │
│ open: No such file or directory                                          │ │
│ [MGA] Couldn't open: /dev/mga_vid                                        │ │
│ [VO_TDFXFB] This driver only supports the 3Dfx Banshee, Voodoo3 and Voodoo 5. │
│ s3fb: Couldn't map S3 registers: Operation not permitted                 │ │
│ Failed to open VDPAU backend libvdpau_nvidia.so: cannot open shared object file: │
│  No such file or directory                                               │ │
│ [vdpau] Error when calling vdp_device_create_x11: 1                       │ │
│ ========================================================================  │ │
│ Opening video decoder: [ffmpeg] FFmpeg's libavcodec codec family         │ │
│ Selected video codec: [ffh264] vfm: ffmpeg (FFmpeg H.264)                │ │
│ ========================================================================  │ │
│ Audio: no sound                                                          │ │
│ FPS forced to be 31.000  (ftime: 0.032).                                 │ │
│ Starting playback...                                                     │ │
│ Movie-Aspect is undefined - no prescaling applied.                       │ │
│ VO: [xv] 1920x1080 => 1920x1080 Planar YV12                              │ │
│ V:   0.0 121/121 234% 35%  0.0% 0 0 0%                                    │ ▣ │
│                                                                          │ │
│ Exiting... (End of file)                                                 │ ▼ │
└──────────────────────────────────────────────────────────────────────────┘
```

Illustration 28

PuTTY for Windows

For our communications you will need PuTTY© installed on your PC. The following describes how to

obtain the PuTTY executable. Go to the main PuTTY Download Page.
http://www.chiark.greenend.org.uk/~sgtatham/putty/download.html. From this page you can select the appropriate file. I suggest you get the Windows installer for everything except PuTTYtel. At this point the latest release is version .63.

Open PuTTY and click on SSH, make appropriate changes.   For Host Name or IP address I am using the IP address (for the Pi) and Port 22. Under Category select (Connection SSH X11) and Enable X11 forwarding. Under Category Session you can name your file under Saved Sessions, which is a real good idea. There are lots of options you set, but we are just using PuTTY to setup our Xming communication so our Python program has a GUI interface.

The PuTTY help files should have been included if things are not working.

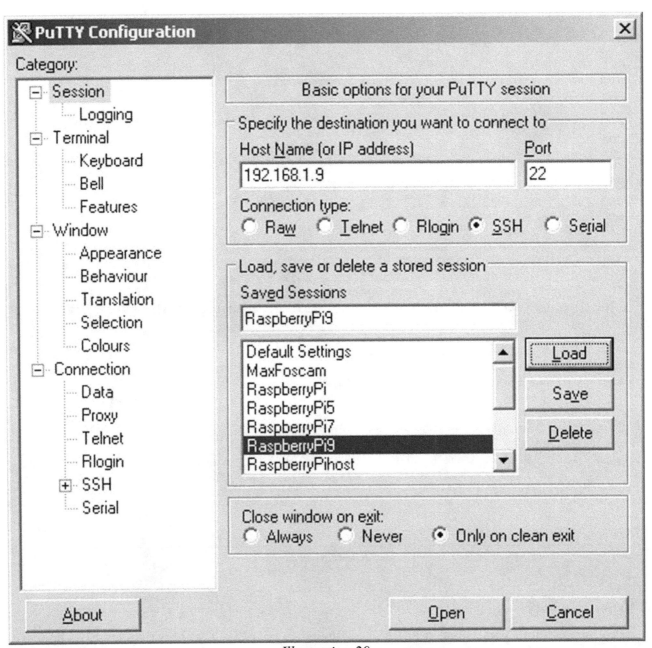

Illustration 29

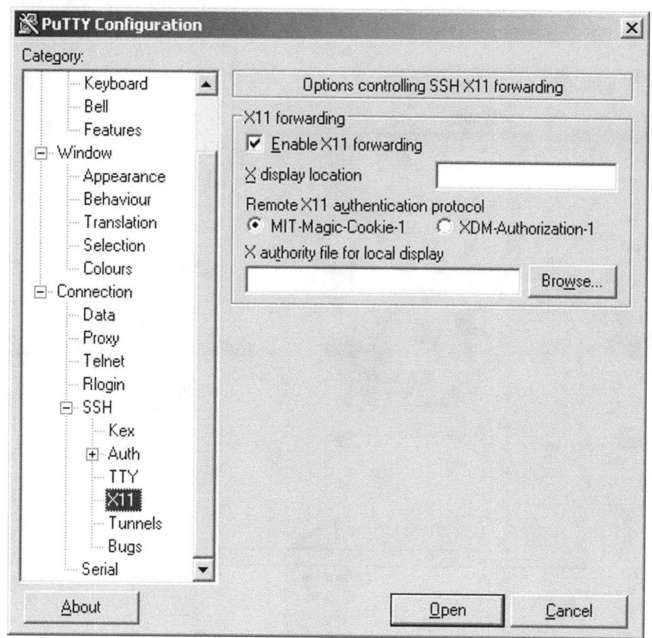

Illustration 30

PuTTY for Debian-Linux

The install is very straight forward. Just run "sudo apt-get install putty". The PuTTY settings are the same as for the Windows version mentioned above. Nice to have but not needed as we will use the standard ssh included with Debian-Linux.

Xming X Server for Windows

This program is needed on your Windows PC to support the GUI interface for our Python Tkinter items. You can download the software from http://sourceforge.net/projects/xming/ . I tried many options, but I think most of my problem in getting it to work was in my not setting up PuTTY. You will need PuTTY for this to work. After you have downloaded Xming you need to run the XLaunch program. I selected "Multiple windows" and on the next screen I selected "Start no client". On the next screen I have checked the "Clipboard" to Start the integrated clipboard manager. On the next screen I saved the configuration and clicked Finish. The Xming server needs to be running on your PC for our Python Tkinter to work.

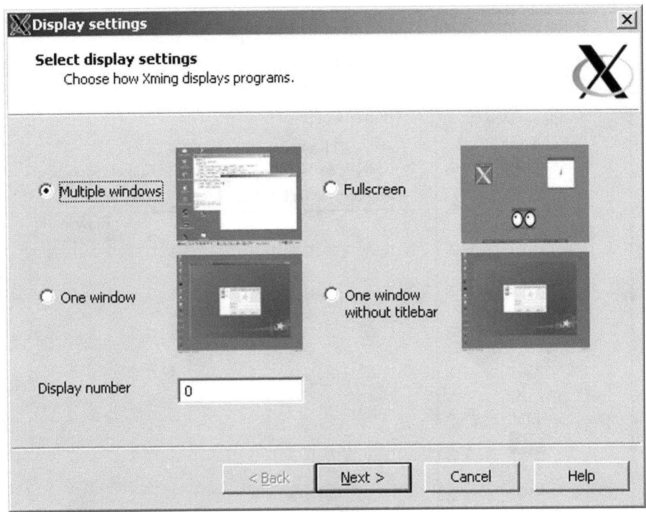

Illustration 31

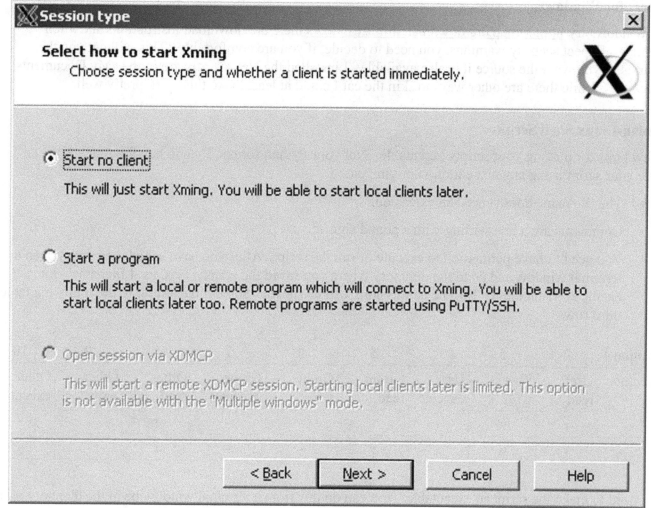

Illustration 32

Geany for Windows

The program has many useful features as well as being a very nice text editor. Go to www.geany.org . The geany-1.2.3.1 setup.exe Full Installer is approximately 8Mb.

Geany for Raspberry Pi

Pretty straight forward enter: "sudo apt-get install geany". If you want to install on the Debian-Linux PC the same command works.

Netcat for Raspberry Pi and Debian-Linux

This is a very neat program but expect to get warning as to security. You should evaluate your system and determine if risk justifies reward. In my case I went for it. You need to install this software on the Raspberry Pi and on your PC.

On Raspberry Pi and your Debian-Linux PC if using that the following command.

sudo apt-get install netcat

The program is also available from http://sourceforge.net/projects/nc110/

Netcat for Windows

On Windows try http://nmap.org/download.html#windows there are download instructions and a self installer. Expect security warnings, you need to decide, if you are comfortable. This will get you the binaries; if you want the source it is also available. I installed the Netcat software in the "My Documents" directory. While there are other ways to skin the cat I could at least make this work pretty well.

Debian-Linux Shell Scripts

A few hints for making your scripts executable. Not your Python scripts, Python handles that. You can write your script using any text editor, vi or vim, etc. I

- The file name doesn't need an extension.

- Comments are a line starting with a pound sign '#'

- You need to have permission to execute or run the script. After you have saved your script open a terminal window and go to the directory where you saved the script. Type 'ls -l filename' for example. (small letter 'L') The permissions will be shown. Something similar to the following table, third row.

position 1	2	3	4	5	6	7	8	9	10
directory flag	User read	User write	User execute	Group read	Group write	Group execute	Other read	Other write	Other execute
-	r	w	-	r	-	-	r	-	-
-	r	w	x	r	-	-	r	-	-

You need to make the script an executable. You can do this from a terminal window be in the directory with your script and type chmod u+x filename. Then retype the ls -l filename and you should see the change as shown on row 4 of the preceding table. (NOTE a small letter L) To run the script from the terminal window, be in the same directory and type. ./filename or type . filename (Notice the . and space)

Debian-Linux Commands

Before using understand that many of the commands have options that are not shown here. For those who may have forgotten some simple Linux commands, a very quick refresher course follows. This is only the tip of the iceberg, just listing a few. Before we go any further, a few quick words on commands. They can do damage, they are not very user friendly; they will destroy without asking twice. So make sure the command you enter is the command that you want and that you know what the command is going to do. Remember when you execute a command that involves a filename you may want to proceed the filename with a "./". Example "cat ./filename".

cat filname	list contents of file
cat filename > filename2	copy filename to filename2
cat /etc/debian_version	this will show what version of Debian you are running
cat /etc/os-release	will show misc. os information
cd	change to home directory
cd /	change to root directory

cd ..	move up one level in the directory tree
chown newower filename	change the owner of filename to the newowner name
chmod u+x filename	example of changing permission of stk500work for the user to execute
clear	clear the screen can also use Ctrl L
cp filename filename2	copy filename to filname2
date	show current day, date and time
df -h	File systems mounted, size, used, avail Use%, where mounted
dmesg	This will show the devices attached, very useful for finding PL2303 and other serial devices attached
echo $SHELL	to see what shell you are running
find -name filename	find the specified filename
free -m	display memory used and free
id	what user you are and what groups you are in
ifconfig	display connections information, (eth0, lo, wlan0, etc)
ip addr show	show connection addresses
kill number	If you need to stop a runaway process, number is the process ID (PID)
lp filename	print filename to default printer
lpstat -t	show default printer
lsusb	list usb devices running on computer
lsusb -v	run as sudo for a complete list, with v is a verbose list
mkdir filename	make a new directory
more filename	list the file, will do in pages
mv filename filname2	move or rename filename to filname2
pwd	to see what your current directory is
whoami	to see what yser you are
ps -p$	generates a process error but shows options
ps -T or ps	show all processes on this terminal
ps -A	show all processes running on computer
ps aux	show all process running on computer, user, PID & more
pstree	show all processes in a tree format
ps -p$$	show current PID TTY TIME CMD
uname -a	display version and kernel
rm filename	delete file specified
reboot	do an immediate shutdown and then reboot
reset	use when console has character map a mess, resets to standard

rmdir directory	remove specified directory
rm -r directory	remove specified directory and contents of the directory
shutdown -h now	shutdown the computer now, you may need sudo in front of command
who	list all users

Reference Sites
The following sites have useful information.

Raspberry

http://www.raspberrypi.org

http://www.element14.com/community/groups/roadtest?ICID=roadtest_subnav

http://www.engadget.com/2012/09/05/cambridge-university-raspberry-pi-guide/

http://www.engadget.com/2012/09/04/raspberry-pi-getting-started-guide-how-to/

http://www.raspberrypi.org/downloads

http://elinux.org/RPiconfig

http://elinux.org/RPi_VerifiedPeripherals

http://elinux.org/RPi_Distributions

http://elinux.org/R-Pi_Troubleshooting

http://elinux.org/RPi_Hardware#Power

http://shallowsky.com/blog/hardware/pi-battery.html

http://elinux.org/RPi_raspi-config

http://asliceofraspberrypi.blogspot.com/2013/05/displaying-system-information-and.html

Raspberry - Camera

http://elinux.org/Rpi_Camera_Module

Xming

http://sourceforge.net/projects/xming/

http://www.straightrunning.com/XmingNotes/pixming.php

Python

www.sourceforge.net
www.docs.python.org
www.astro.ufl.edu
www.sthurlow.com
www.learnpython.org
http://www.astro.ufl.edu/~warner/prog/python.html
www.tutorialspoint.com/python/index.htm
https://developers.google.com/edu/python
http://anh.cs.luc.edu/python/hands-on/handsonHtml/handson.html
http://www.python.org/dev/peps/pep-0008/
http://docs.python.org/2/library/subprocess.html
http://docs.python.org/2/tutorial/errors.html
http://docs.python.org/2/library/stdtypes.html
http://zetcode.com/lang/python/datatypes/

http://www.ibm.com/developerworks/library/os-python1/
http://pguides.net/python-tutorial/python-string-methods/
http://mkaz.com/solog/python-string-format
http://infohost.nmt.edu/tcc/help/pubs/python/web/old-str-format.html
http://www.tutorialspoint.com/python/python_strings.htm
http://docs.python.org/2/library/string.html
http://docs.python.org/2/library/queue.html
http://www.blog.pythonlibrary.org/2012/08/01/python-concurrency-an-example-of-a-queue/
http://stackoverflow.com/questions/2846653/python-multithreading-for-dummies
http://www.tutorialspoint.com/python/python_multithreading.htm
http://docs.python.org/2/library/time.html

Tkinter

http://effbot.org/tkinterbook/grid.htm
http://infohost.nmt.edu/tcc/help/pubs/tkinter/web/index.html
http://www.tkdocs.com/tutorial/windows.html
http://pages.cpsc.ucalgary.ca/~saul/personal/archives/Tcl-Tk_stuff/tcl_examples/
http://effbot.org/tkinterbook/
http://www.pythonware.com/library/tkinter/introduction/hello-tkinter.htm
http://www.tutorialspoint.com/python/python_gui_programming.htm
http://www.beedub.com/book/2nd/TKINTRO.doc.html
http://zetcode.com/gui/tkinter/menustoolbars/
http://effbot.org/tkinterbook/menu.htm
http://infohost.nmt.edu/tcc/help/pubs/tkinter/web/menu.html
http://www.tutorialspoint.com/python/tk_messagebox.htm
http://effbot.org/tkinterbook/canvas.htm
http://www.tutorialspoint.com/python/tk_canvas.htm

Linux

http://steve-parker.org/sh/intro.shtml

http://linuxtutorial.info/modules.php?name=MContent&pageid=329

http://en.wikibooks.org/wiki/Linux_For_Newbies/Command_Line